Front cover and interior Riding Donkey square images by Hodjan.
All other interior illustrations by French caricaturist J. J. Grandville, pseudonym for Jean Ignace Gérard - (1803 – 1847).

Every Image used is in the Public Domain.

FOR FREDERICK

Contents

AMERICAN CORPORATE CULTURE 10
The Annual Office Outing 12
Assertiveness Training 14
The Belt Tightening 16
BENEFITS OF HAVING A MENTOR 18
CANNIBALIZATION 21
CARVING OUT A NICHE UNDER THE PROTECTION OF
THE OLD BOY NETWORK 23
CONSULTANTS OUT 25
CROSS CULTURAL CHIVALRIES 27
DEADWOOD 29
DEMAND FOR TRADE PROTECTION 31
DOWNSIZING 33
ENTITLEMENTS AND THE FEDERAL BUDGET 35
EQUAL PAY FOR EQUAL WORK 37
FLY—BY—NIGHT 39
GET RICH QUICK SCHEME 43
GLOBALIZATION 46
I AM OKAY. YOU ARE NOT SO OKAY 50
INSIDER TRADING 52
INTERNAL COMPETITION 54
INTRAPRENEUR'S LAMENT 57

JOBS 59
THE JOINT VENTURE 63
THE LAW OF SUPPLY AND DEMAND 65
LAYERS OF MANAGEMENT 67
LITIGATION INFLATION 69
MBA DELUSION 71
MEGATRENDS 74
THE MERITS OF FINANCING 76
MYOPIA 78
NEW AND UNIMPROVED PRODUCT PROLIFERATION ... 80
OFFICE POLITICS 82
ON MANAGEMENT STYLES 84
ON THE SHORTFALLS OF MANAGING BY OBJECTIVE .. 86
PAY FOR PERFORMANCE 88
PERSONALITY CLASH 90
THE PRETENDER 93
THE PUBLIC'S IMAGE OF BUSINESS 95
RESTRUCTURING 97
RÉSUMÉ EXPANSION 99
RETURN ON INVESTMENT 101
RULES FOR DEALS 104
SHARK REPELLENT 106
SMALL CAN BE BEAUTIFUL 108

6

STATE OF THE ECONOMY:............................111
THE PERENNIAL VIEW FROM MOUNT OLYMPUS 111
STICK TO THE KNITTING 113
TAX REFORM OR THE MOUNTAIN IN LABOR..........117
TRUTH IS TAKING A BATH 120
WASTE OF TALENT...................................123
Acknowledgements...................................126

WELCOME TO THE SHOW

INTRODUCTORY TIDBITS

To laugh is proper to man.
— Rabelais

A little nonsense now and then
Is relished by the wisest men.

— Anonymous

Never make people laugh. If you
would succeed in life, you must
be solemn, solemn as an ass.
All great monuments are built
over solemn asses.
— Senator Thomas Corwin to
President James Garfield, 1881

AMERICAN CORPORATE CULTURE

Originally, kites had beautiful singing voices. But one day they heard the horses neighing, became envious, and decided to acquire that same skill with the greatest speed.

The desire to learn the neighing of horses became known and spread as quickly as a prairie fire. The kites happened to live in a country inhabited by many creatures of great ingenuity in matters of need recognition and wish fulfillment. Before one could count to three a whole neighing industry had sprung up, with neighing consultants doing a brisk business throughout the land.

At first, the kites attended T-groups to learn neighing. When that did not work they turned to managing by objective, walked around managing, managed quantitatively, synergistically, and even kamikaze-style. As the years went by, they also searched for excellence, adopted the leadership secrets of Attila the Hun, scrambled mightily to manage in One Minute, looked for business wisdom in Sun Tzu's The Art of War, and attempted to earn the trust of a impermanent workforce.

Sadly, in trying to master this competitive new technique of neighing, the swift kites lost the capability they already had: they forgot how to sing. Finally however, the proud birds remembered their roots and decided it was time to go back to basics. Soon, one could watch all the kites taking singing lessons. The song of the month had lyrics on how one empowered employees without giving them a raise or health insurance. Only here and there could one see a few clever birds wondering what there was left to learn, and what they could sell next.

By Fashion taught.....
Fashion, that prudence sometimes overrules
But serves instead of reason to the fools!
Fashion, which all the world to slavery brings,
The dull excuse for doing silly things.

— *John Wilmot, Earl of Rochester*

The Annual Office Outing

A wolf that had been careless enough to swallow a bone at the merry company picnic went about looking for a creature to relieve him of it. Mingling with the rank and file he met a heron and made a deal with him. The bird would remove the bone and the wolf would grant him a favor in return.

Fearlessly, the heron put his long beak and his entire head between the wolf's sharp teeth and down his throat. Then he was able to pull out the bone.

Not wanting to seem too eager, the heron waited for a few days before visiting the wolf in his fancy corner office. After the exchange of some pleasant small talk, he said to the wolf: "I am ready for the promotion you promised me." The wolf displayed a toothy grin and answered: "Is it your habit to take silly things said during social gatherings at face value? You should be content, my friend, with having gotten your head safe and sound out of the wolf's mouth. That's a privilege! I would not advise you to demand a reward as well."

Botticelli isn't a wine, Juggins!
Botticelli is a cheese!

— *Punch, 1895*

It is dangerous to be sincere,
Unless you are also stupid.

— *George Bernard Shaw*

The only way to treat a Prussian
Is to step on his toes
Until he apologizes.

— *Anonymous*

Assertiveness Training

A garden snake was trodden on by so many so-workers that it went to Zeus and complained about it.

"I did it all," said the snake. " I have been Mr. Nice Guy as long as I can remember. I have been the perfect team-player, and I am certainly not what you would call a problem employee. And for all that, nobody shows me any respect or appreciation!"

"Too bad," answered Zeus, "that you failed to do one thing that is necessary: if you had bitten the first animal that trod on you, the next one would have thought twice about stepping on you."

*'Tis strange how over-nice are some
About their work, their manners, and their fun,
While what's of worth they slightly pass it by
Not doing it at all, or slovenly.*

— *John Bunyan*

*So well-bred Spaniels civilly delight
In mumbling of the game they dare not bite.*

— *Alexander Pope*

The Belt Tightening

The chairman of the wolves had established a policy stipulating that each of them should accept a number of cut-backs in perquisites, bonuses, and salaries for the good of their troubled firm; so that they should not be driven by the hunger of retrenchment to tear at each other's throats.

But one of the mules working under the management of the wolves came forward, and shaking his gray mane, addressed the chairman as follows:

"Out of the mind of the wolf has come a noble thought. It is wise to set a good example. It gives us mules a reason to put up with wage-and benefit cuts, and even with layoffs. But how is it, Mr. Wolf, that you yourself laid up in your den the fat quarry you got hold of recently? Put it in the company piggy bank where it belongs."

This exposure shamed the wolf into annulling the belt-tightening policy for wolves in general, and into designing a just-in-case severance package for himself in particular. It was the most beautiful and sublime golden parachute ever engineered by man or beast.

This plain distinction, Sir, so doubt secures,
'Tis not true reason I despise, but yours.

— *John Wilmot, Earl of Rochester*

Sir, are you so grossly ignorant of human nature as not to know that a man may be very sincere in good principles without having good practice?

— *Samuel Johnson*

BENEFITS OF HAVING A MENTOR

An executive purchased a parrot to which he gave the run of the offices.

It was quite tame, and jumping one day onto the water cooler outside the executive's suite, it perched there and kept up a cheerful chatter.

The office cat eyed it, and asked who it was and where it came from. It said the boss had just bought it from the competition and was grooming it for better things to come.

"Then most audacious of creatures," said the cat, "imagine a newcomer like you making such a noise, when I, who was born and raised in these offices, am not allowed a single meow! If ever I do, management is annoyed, and chases me away,"

"Oh mistress of the office," answered the parrot, " my advice is that you take early retirement or keep your meows to yourself. You see, there is a difference: this corporate community does not dislike my voice as it does yours."

I am his Highness' dog at Kew;
Pray tell me, Sir, whose dog are you?

— *Alexander Pope*

Ambition often puts men upon the meanest
Offices; so climbing is performed in the
Same posture as creeping.

— *Jonathan Swift*

CANNIBALIZATION

Once upon a time a goat named New Bubblewater and an ass named Old Bubblewater were busy serving the same large corporation. The goat, New Bubblewater, grew jealous because the ass, Old Bubblewater, was highly regarded as a cash cow and had an enormous advertising budget at his disposal with plenty of cash to spare.

One day the goat had a bright idea, came to the ass and said "Old Bubblewater, your life is a never-ending toil, what with being an American symbol like working motherhood and store-bought apple pie! I recommend that you have a fit and tumble into a hole so that you have a well-earned rest. I, New Bubblewater, am your friend. Let me carry part of the burden for a while. It stays in the family."

The ass took the advice, tumbled into a hole, and was injured by the fall.

So the Board of Directors called for the veterinary surgeons and requested their help. The physicians prescribed broth made from the goat's innards, which they said would result in a cure. So they cut up the goat to nurture the ass back to health.

*Life is a jest, and all things show it,
I thought so once, and now I know it.*

— *John Gay*

Some are wise, and some are otherwise.

— *Anonymous*

CARVING OUT A NICHE UNDER THE PROTECTION OF THE OLD BOY NETWORK

An entrepreneurial lark once made his nest in the lush cornfield of a market leader and fed his young on its tender shoots till they had crests on their heads and were fully fledged. One day, when the market leader inspected his domain he saw that the crop was dry, ripe, and mature. "It's time now," he said, "to call in my supporting friends to help me with the reaping."

One of the lark's bright chicks heard him and alerted his father, bidding him to move on. "There is no need to think of going yet for a while" replied the lark. "The man who trusts his cronies to do a necessary thing in a great hurry is in no great hurry about it."

When the market leader came again and saw the ears of the corn dropping off under the hot sun of competition, he said that now he must hire reapers and sheaf carriers the next day.

"We have grown well in this cornfield," said the lark to his offspring. "Now it is really time for us to move, when the great leader relies on himself instead of on his so-called friends."

Sir Stafford has a brilliant mind, until it is made up.

— *Lady Violet Bonham Carter*

There was a Rich Man who said "Hush!
I perceive a young bird in this bush!"
When they said "Is it small?" he replied "Not at all!
It's grown four times as big as the bush!"

— *Edward Lear*

CONSULTANTS OUT

A cat heard from a reliable source that there were sick hens on a rich farm.

So he dressed himself up as a doctor and presented himself there as an expert on bird flu. He carried a large bag filled with impressive professional regalia, instruments, and learned studies done about other hens at other rich farms.

Outside the sumptuous farmhouse he stood and called out to the hens, asking them how they were, "Fine" came the reply, "if you get off the premises."

*Things are seldom what they seem,
Skim milk masquerades as cream.*

— *W.S. Gilbert*

*For every ill beneath the sun,
There is a remedy, or none.
Should there be one resolve to find it.
If not, submit, and never mind it.*

— *Anonymous*

CROSS CULTURAL CHIVALRIES

Once upon a time a foreign dragon came to visit an American eagle and they traveled together through the United States. The conversations were conducted in fluent Eaglise English.

The eagle of course was on home ground and proudly presented his great country to the guest. By the roadside stood a block of stone on which was carved the image of an eagle throttling a dragon. The host pointed a sly finger at it and said: "You see, we Yankees know how to be on top of things!"

A smile flickered across the dragon's face and he replied: "How elegantly tactful of you to show me this masterpiece! But I will say that if dragons cared to carve, you would often observe a dragon pinning down an eagle if you came to visit my country. But as it is, we are more interested in exporting than in carving.

This is why I visit your country able to communicate and negotiate in fluent Eaglise. Do you speak Dragonese? No? Or French, Spanish, Arabic, Russian, German and Japanese? Neither? Well, we do. Perhaps it would be beneficial for you to brush up on international business etiquette and on languages as an alternative to showing off monuments carved during a past age of innocence. I seem to remember that your balance of payments has room for improvement."

*How much a dunce that has been sent to roam
Excels a dunce that has been kept at home!*
— William Cowpter

*How little are our customs known
On this side of the herring-pond!*
— John Gay

*Besides men there are Saxons and Americans,
But we won't take them up until next year,
When we have Zoology.*
— Kurt Tucholsky

DEADWOOD

A blacksmith had a dog which slept while he worked but stood by his side when he ate. The dog complained loudly that the compensation and benefits in this declining industry were insufficient and that he could not live on the scraps he received — considering that he was always punctual and had no record of absenteeism.

"Sleepy wretch," said the smith as he threw him a bone. "When I strike the anvil and work like a dog to stay alive in this business with structural difficulties, you go to bed. But when I get my teeth into action to have a well- deserved meal, you're soon awake."

If little labor, little are our gains;
Man's fortunes are, sometimes,
According to his pains.

— Robert Herrick

He that would thrive
Must rise at five,
He that has thriven,
May lie till seven.

— John Clarke

DEMAND FOR TRADE PROTECTION

A lion was continually finding fault with Prometheus and complained loudly that without protection against marauders ruining his trade, he would soon be on the endangered species list. It was true that Prometheus had made him big and handsome, and armed his jaws with teeth and his paws with claws, and had given him greater strength than any other animal, but despite all these advantages he was afraid of cocks.

These belligerent beasts constantly intruded into his territory, chased the game and his customers away, and as a result he had to stay hungry.

"You have no reason to blame me," replied Prometheus. "You have everything that I could give you, every gift it was in my power to fashion for you. It is your own spirit that creates this weakness."

At this the lion was disappointed, and kept accusing himself of cowardice, till at length he felt a terrible pity for himself, and fell into apathy. But while he was in this frame of mind he met an elephant, greeted him, and stopped for a talk.

He noticed that the elephant kept moving his ears all the time. "What's the matter," he asked, "can't you keep your ears still for a moment so that we can talk in peace?"

Just then, a swarm of gnats happened to fly around the elephant's head.

"Do you see these nasty, buzzing things?" asked the elephant. "The current economic climate favors them. I can't hold my ears still for even a minute. If they get into the passage of my ears, it's all over with me. But they won't. I am on guard."

"Well," said the lion. "If such a mighty animal like you is in danger, there is no need for me to give up. It was pleasant talking to you. Good luck."

As the lion trotted on, he said to himself : "Prometheus refuses to bargain. But I am big and strong, and more fortunate than the elephant who is afraid of tiny things. At any rate, a cock is something to be more afraid of than a gnat."

So, naturalists observe, the flea
Hath smaller fleas that on him prey;
And these have smaller fleas to bite 'em,
And so proceed, ad infinitum.
— *Jonathan Swift*

As soon as I have asserted a proposition:
Where can more examples be found?
— *Lichtenberg*

DOWNSIZING

A sheep was being shorn left-handedly and knew it. For months it had gagged when asked to swallow the latest sanitary announcements about reorganization, restructuring, and reengineering, plus the puffery on the great value in which the company held its employees.

Soon it was exposed to the outplacement (firing squad) consultants hired by the concerned corporation to enhance the image of social responsibility and to shield upper management from having to face the job loss casualties man to man and woman to woman.

Companies signed up for these services as a hypocrisy insurance policy.

Before long, the sacrificial lamb understood that these outplacement consultants operated to lighten some of the financial burdens shouldered by the corporation as it eliminated the workers from the payroll.

A day came when the sheep decided it had enough. "Listen," it said. "If it is my wool you want, don't cut so close. It hurts. But if it is my flesh you are after, get it over with and don't cut me up by inches."

*In things a moderation keep
Employers ought to shear
Not skin their sheep.*

— Robert Herrick (modified by E. Schelby)

*He that complies against his will,
Is of his own opinion still.*

— Samuel Butler

ENTITLEMENTS AND THE FEDERAL BUDGET

The rivers from all the states in the Union gathered together and complained against the surrounding sea. "We bring you all of our resources, our strength, and the creatures living on our shores work for months to pay high tributes to you," said the rivers.

"Why is it, when we enter your big waters fresh and rich with nutrients, that you dissolve us and turn us into salt, or, heaven forbid, even into foul smelling Algae Blooms?"

Hearing itself thus blamed, the sea replied: "Rich with nutrients? You mean toxic run-offs from your industrial farms and feeding lots? So don't run to the ocean if you wish to stop the cycle of pollution plus the evaporation that brings the rain of entitlements to the lands through which you flow."

> O let us love our occupations,
> Bless Congress and its reparations;
> Live upon our daily rations,
> And always know our proper stations.
>
> — Charles Dickens, modified by E. Schelby

> April 15:
> I made it known by proclamation,
> Today is no feast day in this nation,
> Wherefore this day forever may
> Be fêted as Nonholiday.
>
> — Christian Morgenstern

> More spending begets the desire for more;
> The hunger still increases with the store.
>
> — Dryden

> What nature requires is obtainable and within easy reach.
> It's for the superfluous we sweat.
>
> — Seneca

EQUAL PAY FOR EQUAL WORK

The hares were unhappy with their lot and decided to address a big public meeting.

There they passionately claimed that all animals should have equal pay for doing equally or comparably difficult work.

The lions answered: "A fine speech, Hairy Feet, but it lacks claws and teeth such as we have."

Details are always vulgar.

— *Oscar Wilde.*

All the men on my staff can type.

— *Bella Abzug*

My advice to the women's clubs of America is to raise more hell and fewer dahlias.

— *William Allen White*

FLY—BY—NIGHT

In a dispute between the ant and the fly, the latter boasted:

"I have," said he, "all the advantages of selling competitive foreign products under my own well-known brand-name without having the burden of producing them domestically.

No capital investments for plant and equipment, no labor problems, no costs for health insurance and retirement benefits, reduced overhead, market-driven flexibility, and increasing profits! Why should we do it expensively at home, if it can be done abroad with cheap labor? Wall Street loves us!"

The ant said nothing. The fly continued: "In comparison, look at you, you poor, flat-footed drudge, Crawling around in the dirt, living in holes, supporting a big labor-force, and huffing and puffing from constant exertion while gathering up some meager earnings to justify a wretched existence! Look at your production facilities! A pile of rubble! And have you seen your new corporate headquarters, done by architect Copyos Bauhaus the XX?"

"Hogwash, you flimsy fly," said the ant. "I pretend to none of your cleverness or peculiar corporate style. Doing well on Wall Street, living off the fat of your company's brand-name, exploiting today as if there is no tomorrow might suit a flighty thing like you, but it will not do for me. I do what I can, I am regarded as an example of prudence and foresight. I don't believe in the quick-fix, and I don't like excessive short-cuts. Neither do I court favors, nor dread the frowns of anyone or anything. In contrast, your marvelous opportunities turn you into a parasitic intruder who is buzzing around wherever he can get a present supply. You may sip honey today, but soon you will feed on carrion; and having propagated a numerous progeny, equally noxious and useless as yourself, your magnificent headquarters will turn into a fly-trap. It will be nothing but a hollow pomposity. And you know what? Your suppliers will learn, and will use you as fishing bait before you know it. You are already dangling at the end of a sharp hook. Your marketing savvy is fine for a while, but you will degenerate into a redundant middleman – forgive me, middlefly – and then let's see if Wall Street is fickle!

Thus encounter happened shortly before the Covid pandemic arrived, disrupted global trade, and messed up all the supply chains.

Minimal encumberments
Will be best for his intends.

— *Wilhelm Busch*

I remember when our whole island was shaken with an earthquake some years ago, there was an impudent mountebank who sold pills which where good against earthquake.

— *Joseph Addison*

Why has not man a microscopic eye?
For this plain reason, Man is not a fly.

—*Alexander Pope*

When an economic problem and a head collide and there is a hollow sound, is it always the fault of of the economic problem?

— *Lichtenberg; paraphrased by E. Schelby*

GET RICH QUICK SCHEME

A financial adviser had taken his own recommendations too seriously and found himself in a temporary position of negative cash-flow. As a remedy, he made a wooden statue of Hermes and took it to market with the intention to sell.

Unfortunately, no buyer could be found. So the adviser decided to conduct a marketing campaign by snail mail, email, and twitter. Soon he shouted in his letters and miniblogs that he had a god for sale, a god who showered blessings on anyone who made the purchase: Hermes would make the customer rich - overnight.

"Oh will he?" said a Fox, calling him up. "If the god of gain can perform such wonderful deeds, why do you want to sell him? Why don't you keep him for yourself and get fat and juicy profits through his help?"

"But it is ready cash that I need, right now," replied the exasperated financial adviser, "and it takes Hermes an awfully long time to put profits into one's pocket."

No one bull-dog yet could eat
Any other bull-dog's meat;
If you have a good-sized bone,
Let the other dog alone.

— *Anonymous*

You are an informer, a calumniator, a forger, a secret agent, a slave to the unclean, and a trainer of gladiators. I wonder, Vacerra, why you have no money.

— *Martial*

GLOBALIZATION

It is rumored that this has happened before: anyway, one day the belly and the members of the world-body argued which of them was right and made the greatest contribution to international trade, to the smooth functioning of the economic interaction around the globe, and to the common good.

All the members trumpeted loudly about their own sacrifices made for the well-being of the global community. Before long, consensus was reached that the incurably gluttonous belly was the major offender among them.

The tongue was appointed spokes-organ. Aggravating the grievances of the members, he set out to deliver numerous seditious speeches to the media and to delegates of international organizations. Meanwhile, the other members continued to have discussions among themselves, disregarding the official consensus they had adopted. Each of them praised the activities, diligence, and wisdom of its own actions, and disparaged the doings of others. Yet despite all of these sportive amusements, nobody forgot to blame the real villain, the corpulent belly.

Yes, he was insatiable, complained the hands. And not only that, sneered the feet.

After stuffing himself, gobbling up resources, goods, and capital, he fell into the disruptive habit of going on one financial fad-diet after another — all of which usually ended badly. Exactly, said the backside, he is unpredictable and selfish. During his periods of fierce fasting I am forced to shrink down to nothing. He blows me up or deflates me according to his whim.

Thus continued the chorus of the members, setting forth how hard and unreasonable it was that the fruits of their economic efforts, labor, and fiscal policy should all be squandered away upon the cravings of a fat and indolent paunch.

In short, it was resolved for the future to stop any economic interaction with the belly and to let him shift for himself as well as he could. The hands protested they would not lift a finger for his service any longer. The teeth refused to chew a single morsel for his use. The feet mocked that he would end up immobilized because they would no longer carry him about.

The belly remonstrated in vain; for during the clamor of passion nobody listens to reason. Finally, the stomach had had enough and said: "Do as you wish and see where you end up. Nature has made me so that I will survive pretty well. I will just shrink. Of course I understand that you have fun with blaming the belly. It's all my fault, no matter what — too much or too little, too soon or too late. Whatever. Live with it."

So the unnatural resolution was kept as long as anything of that kind can be kept, which was, until each of the members had wasted away to skin and bones or less, and could hold out no longer.

Then they decided there was no doing without the belly, and that, if he could only be a little less of a glutton, he would still contribute to the welfare of all the other parts, just as they aided, according to their stations, his maintenance.

Having grown scrawny and weak, all the members of the world body presently scrambled to institute a new policy of cooperation, which, they now agreed eagerly, was necessary to nurse them all back to health. For a while at least, nobody was anti-belly anymore. Until a big bubble burst, but that is another story.

Some neither can for wits or critics pass,
As heavy mules are neither horse or ass.

— *Alexander Pope*

Just as philosophy is the study of other people's misconceptions, so history is the study of other people's mistakes.

— *Philip Guedalla*

Tis evident beasts are, in their decree,
As wise at least, and better far than he.
Those creatures are the wisest who attain
By surest means the ends at which they aim.
If therefore Jowler finds, and kills, his hares
Better than Presidents supply committee chairs;

Though one is a statesman, th'other but a hound
Jowler in justice will be wiser found.

—*John Wilmot, Earl of Rochester*

When myth meets myth, the collision is very real.

—Stanislev Lec

*In this world he muses sadly,
There is much that functions badly.*

—Wilhelm Busch
transl. Walter Arndt

I AM OKAY. YOU ARE NOT SO OKAY

A lion was busy working on an ambitious project and invited an ass to help him with achieving the desired results of eliminating some unwanted competition by hostile takeover. Both beasts walked to a large cave in which there were some wild goats that had to be driven out and subdued.

The lion decided to stand at the cave entrance and watch for the tasty goats to come out, while the ass was given the job of entering the cave and charging into their midst with the loudest braying he was capable of.

The lion caught all the goats. Then the ass came running out and asked excitedly if he hadn't put up a good show at scaring these dumb animals half to death and driving them out. "I give you my word," replied the lion, "I should have been frightened of you myself if I hadn't known you were an ass."

You must stir it and strump it,
And blow your trumpet,
Or trust me, you haven't a chance.

— W.S. Gilbert

There is so much good in the worst of us,
And so much bad in the best of us,
That it hardly becomes any of us,
To talk about the rest of us.

— E.W. Hoch

INSIDER TRADING

A wolf was busy carrying to his lair a sheep he had lifted from his employer's holdings when a lion met him and took it from him.

Standing at a safe distance, the wolf voices his protest: "You have no right to take away what is mine. Give it back, I need it urgently!"

"Of course you need it, my friend," replied the lion. "I know you came by it quite rightfully. I have no doubt that it was a bonus from your friendly employer supplementing your salary, which is much too meager for a fellow with your inventive genius."

Industrious pirate! See him sweep
The lonely bosom of the deep,
And daily the horizon scan
From Hatteras to Far Japan,
Be sure, before the pirate's old,
He will have made a pot of gold,
And will retire from his labors
And be respected by his neighbors.
You also scan your life's horizon
For all that you can clap your eyes on.

— Robert Louis Stevenson

It is no good hen that cackles in your house and lays in another's.

—Anonymous

Sir, I do not know whether you will die on the gallows or of the pox. That will depend, my Lord, on whether I embrace your principles or your mistress.

— John Wilkes

INTERNAL COMPETITION

A crow sat high and pretty on the corporate ladder holding in his beak a juicy piece of the department he had just taken away from an internal competitor.

A fox, who was also eager to engage in empire building by stepping on the turf of the guy in the next corner office, saw the crow and was determined to get the meaty department for himself. Standing under the ladder he began to tell the crow what a dynamic big bird he was, how elegantly he was dressed in his shiny black coat, and that it was clear to everyone that he would advance to becoming the eagle-eyed leader of the entire aviary. Undoubtedly, the fox argued, a crow of his caliber would already have been made top flyer of the entire bird division if only he had a commanding voice as well. How about a little voice training or instruction in public speaking?

The crow was so eager to prove that he had a good voice that he opened his beak, dropped the meaty department, and croaked for all he was worth. Up ran the fox, snapped up the big fat morsel on the run, and said to his hapless competitor: " Too bad that you can't add some intelligence to all your other qualifications. I'm afraid you don't have what it takes.

*Thou shalt not covet: but tradition
Approves all forms of competition.*

— A.H.Clough

*Nature made every fop to plague his brother
Just as one beauty mortifies another.*

— Alexander Pope

GOING TO THE BANQUET.

INTRAPRENEUR'S LAMENT

A bird in a gilded cage sang only after working hours. A lean bat, roaming around freely in the dark, heard him and asked why a bird with his abilities sang at night, and not in the morning, and all day long, as he should.

The bird explained that there was a good reason: his employer had encouraged him to sing joyous entrepreneurial songs during the daytime ever since the company had decided to promote creativity and innovation by establishing an exemplary intrapreneurial program. He had done this, and came up with many bold new songs.

At first management had not liked any of them, but then, suddenly, it saw value in them. So he was captured and put into a golden cage. This had taught him a lesson. Unfortunately, he was now no longer able to sing during his working hours, when the sun was up.

"It's no good to be sorry now," said the bat. "You should have been aware of the cage. You should have spread your wings. You could have flown off on your own before you mistook intrapreneurial tunes for entrepreneurial songs."

There once was a man who said 'Damn!
It is born upon me I am
An engine that moves
In predestinate grooves,
I'm not even a bus, I'm a tram.'

— Maurice Evan Hare

A Robin Redbreast in a cage
Puts all Heaven in a rage.

— William Blake

JOBS

Once upon a time, a frog observed a strong ox plowing a field, pulling a wagon, and going to market with his master. At the end of each day, the ox always ate a scrumptious meal, rested in a well-maintained stable, and enjoyed good healthcare from a veterinarian.

The next time the frog watched this particular oxen at his work the said with a sneer: "what an outdated way to earn a living. Your bulk and muscle power have become an anachronism in the post-industrial era. There are fewer and fewer jobs for beasts like you!"

"Get out of my way, you wimpy little varmint," growled the ox. The frog jumped a pace. "Moron," he squawked. "You and your ilk don't count any longer. Manufacturing has shown a steady decline, and corporate agribusinesses have changed farming beyond recognition. These days, we have free trade around the globe. Everything manufactured is being made by the little dragons, the big dragons, and other clever animals. Besides, you are too humongous. You eat too much. Your upkeep is far too expensive. It's much cheaper to feed less massive critters far away, across our oceans and borders. As for the good old home country, have you ever heard of the service-economy? And the information society? That's where it's at. I am in it. It's large, and it's growing. Look at me!"

So the frog blew up his body until all the wrinkles and folds disappeared. Then he called out to all the other frogs in the fast food, fast coffee, and hospitality establishments, the discount stores, and the financial and digital services establishments to come on over and do the same thing.

"Aren't we bigger and fatter than you?" asked the leader of the frogs. "No" replied the ox. "You are just full of hot air. Now leave me alone and stop your blather. I have work to do. Someone has to do the real stuff around here."

"This just shows what a dumb brute you are," said the frog. Then he ordered all his companions to blow even more and to puff themselves up to a size that would leave no doubt about their importance. Combined they would be many times bigger than the ox and his labor-intensive comrades.

Their combined size would show that fact.

Sure enough, all the frogs made frantic efforts to swell themselves up out of all proportion. But after a new millennium came along, they finally had so much air in their little bodies that they exploded with a great big bang in a great big bust. The noise was so loud it could be heard on Wall Street and all across the big pond in the fine City of London.

Now here, you see, it takes all the running you can do, to keep in the same place. If you want to get somewhere else, you must run at least twice as fast.
— *Lewis Carroll*

The length of this line shows the ton of coal as dug by the miner.
This one shows the ton shipped to the dealer.
The small dealer gets a ton like this.
This is the one you pay for.
This is what you get.
The residue is:
Cinders and
Ashes.
This last line will give you some idea about the size of the bill.

— *Anonymous*

THE JOINT VENTURE

A fox tumbled into a water tank and could not get out. Along came a thirsty goat who asked him if the water was good.

The fox jumped at the chance to employ his guile. He sang the praises of the water with all the eloquence at his command. "Just think of the business potential," he said.

"Consumers have a love-affair with health enhancing waters ever since two-Martini lunches became passé! All we need to do is fill the water into nice bottles, affix a label that has snob appeal, and sell under an upscale concept. The cost of entry is almost zero: we can make a fortune on it! It would even help the balance of payments — buy American I say. Why should we import mere water from the frilly French, when we have it right here!"

The goat became even thirstier as he listened to this splendid presentation. "Come on down," said the fox, and the goat went down without stopping to think, and drank his fill.

"Let's talk about a joint venture, "said the fox. "First, we have to get out of here, then we can start planning for our bottling business. You can help by earning sweat-equity. Be so kind and place your fore-feet against the wall and hold your horns straight up. Then I can climb up, and pull you out too." The goat was glad enough to comply. The fox clambered nimbly over his haunches, shoulders, and horns, reached the edge of the tank and began to make off. The goat was trapped in the tank and complained that their agreement had been broken.

But the fox came only back to mock him: "you have more hair in your beard than brains in your head, my friend. Otherwise you wouldn't have jumped in without figuring out how to get out. You are an ideal target for friendly financial swindlers."

Sad to say, there is not a virtue
I can ever have much fun with;
Always I am at my easiest
When that business is done with.

Quite conversely, it is vices
That agree with me, I find:
Pleasant little jobs I'd rather
See before me than behind.
   —Wilhelm Busch, translation Walter Arndt

The fox changes his fur,
But not his habits.

— *Suetonius*

THE LAW OF SUPPLY AND DEMAND

A race horse and an ass were traveling with their superior on business. The race horse was a fast talker and had the knack of shirking work with the greatest ease.

"Take a share of my load if you want to save me from a coronary," said the overburdened ass to his colleague.

But the horse, who prided himself on his looks, his gamesmanship, and his brains, would not. "Work smarter, not harder," he replied.

The ass, worn out by doing too much from dawn to dusk, for seventy hours per week, succumbed to fatigue, fell down, died, and satisfied the statistics predicting just that for beasts of burden.

"He was a fine employee of the old school," said the superior. "And an example of the new productivity, too. Did the work of three. I once saw him handle five phones simultaneously. Well, but now we are short-footed, and this job needs to be done." So without delay the boss put the whole load on the horse's sleek back, with the ass's hide into the bargain.

The horse began to groan and set up a piteous lament. "Alas," he cried, "what misery I let myself in for! I would not take a light load off the ass's back and now look at me! Now I have to carry everything, hide and all!"

Toil, says the proverb,
   Is the sire of fame.

— *Euridipes*

Of all the lunacies earth can boast
The one that must please the devil most
Is pride reduced to the whimsical terms
Of causing the slugs to despise the worms.

—*Brough*

"There's been an accident!" they said,
"Your servant is cut in half, he's dead!"
"Indeed!" said Mr. Jones, "and please
Send me the half that's got my keys."

— *Harry Graham*

LAYERS OF MANAGEMENT

A company trained one of its best hounds to go out hunting for sales orders but it kept all the other animals as house dogs.

These home-based dogs were so busy evaluating, distributing, processing, and managing orders that not one of them had time for customers. A complicated voice mail system guided each caller through a maze of options, thereby stealing the customer's time. That unfortunate creature never encountered the live bark of a corporate house dog. Even if the customer knew a special extension number, the animal in question couldn't be reached. Whenever one of these nuisances called, a growling voice mail message announced that the wanted dog was away from his desk and that the call would be returned as soon as possible.

The hunting dog complained bitterly because whenever he caught game in the sales chase, all the domesticated dogs were given a large share of it.

"It is not fair" he barked, "that I have to go out and have such a tough time of it, while this entire staff and all those lap dogs at headquarters grow fat on the fruits of my labors simply by shuffling computer print-outs."

"Dear hound, don't blame us" said the dogs. "Blame the company, or better yet the system, for both never taught us to hunt for ourselves. For us it is quite normal to live from the prey that others bring in."

On hearing this, the hunting hound quit and immediately started his own business.

Marketing Research Manager: I lost my briefcase
Salesman: I pity your grief.
Marketing Research Manager: My tabulations are in it.
Salesman: I pity the thief.

—Anonymous

But thoughts were given for action's government
Where action ceases, thought is impertinent.

— John Wilmot, Earl of Rochester

LITIGATION INFLATION

A wolf, who was trained as an attorney and specialized in tort law, strolled along a river and saw a fine, plump lamb drinking from it. With his appetite aroused, he decided to devour the lamb in one way or another.

Standing higher up on the stream, the wolf accused the lamb of polluting the water through the unclean manufacturing of wool. The lamb said that he was only drinking with the tip of his tongue, that his wool business was perfectly natural and without harm to the environment, and that he could not possibly muddy the water for His Honor the Wolf simply because he stood at a location downstream from that legal predator.

"Evasions are unacceptable" said the wolf. "It does not matter in the least where you stand, it only matters that you pollute the river for everyone by drinking and by dropping pieces of your chemically dangerous wool in it. I am going to show that your covering is not natural at all, but carcinogenic." "But I could accuse you of the same thing" said the exasperated lamb, "you have a mouth and a hairy coat too!"

"That is not the issue" replied the wolf. "I am going to construct a case against you and get into the deep pockets of your expensive pure wool coat, and that's that. Not only do you muddy the water, you also slandered my client's father last year and your wool products caused severe allergies and intense suffering to a whole group of my clients since last spring. We will sue you for damages you never heard or dreamed of."

"But this is utterly absurd," said the lamb. "I wasn't even born then!"

"You are good in finding answers," said the wolf, but did you ever hear about original sin? Your species was involved in it, and I will get you on that. You can say whatever you want, but you are going to be eaten up all the same."

> *"Virtue in the middle," said the Devil*
> *as he seated himself between two lawyers.*
> — *Anonymous*

> *Even a wolf will not stay*
> *Where sounds no bleat to offer hope of prey.*
> — *Greek epigram*

> *Justice while she winks at crimes,*
> *Stumbles on innocence sometimes.*
> — *Samuel Butler*

MBA DELUSION

A young wolf freshly graduated from a prestigious business school wandered around the headquarters of a large investment bank when he observed the long shadow cast by his body.

"Now why on earth should a fabulous fellow like me be impressed by a lion," he said to himself. "Gee, I must be thirty feet long! Who cares about just another market crash: a capable beast must think big. I'll seek empowerment by making myself king on the fast-track, and I'll control all these billions of dollars, and rule over all these corporate animals, every one of them!"

But despite all his boasting, a powerful lion caught the young wolf by the throat and kicked him out into the slow lane.

"I should have made a meal out of you," growled the lion. "So down with you! Count your blessings and lots of tedious little beans in the back office. Learn to get your numbers straight. The regulations have been tightened. Move. To the basement with you!"

Too late, the wolf regretted his hubris. "Conceit," he wailed," has helped to make a ruin of my brilliant career."

*A young Apollo, golden-haired,
Stands dreaming at the verge of strife,
Magnificently unprepared
For the long littleness of life.*

— *F.C. Cornford*

*He rose in less than half an hour,
To riches, dignity, and power.*

— *Hilaire Belloc*

MEGATRENDS

After Zeus fashioned men, he called for Hermes and said to him: "These clever mortals are already busy inventing bureaucracy. As god of profit and trade, that's your department. Go down to them, and endow each organization and each institution with effectiveness."

Hermes was glad to take care of the request. He made a vessel for measuring the precious essence of effectiveness and poured an equal quantity of it into each emerging organization. It was enough to fill all the little firms and institutions quite full, and they buzzed along nicely and became effective.

But the amount originally measured out by Hermes remained constant and was soon too small to percolate through the bodies of huge organizations in business and government, which all grew gigantic under the machinations of their administrators over time. As a result, these dinosaurs suffered from sclerosis and became rather ineffective.

*Fix'd like a plant on its peculiar spot
To draw nutrition, propagate, and rot.*

— *Alexander Pope*

In a world full of problems, he sat doing puzzles.

—*Kenneth Burke*

*He was busy, he was needed!
You could see him everywhere,
Trade affairs or civic functions:
He was active, he was there.
Nothing could be done without him,
He was always on the go.
Yesterday, when he was buried,
Yes, you guessed it: he did show.*

—*Wilhelm Busch, transl. Dieter P. Lotze*

THE MERITS OF FINANCING

A fox had started a company and slipped in climbing the fence of rapid, uncontrolled growth. To save himself he clutched at a tough brier bush operating as a financial firm.

The brier bush financier stopped his downfall, but its large thorns made his paws bleed, and in his pain the fox cried out: "Oh dear, I turned to you for help and you made me worse off than I was before."

"Yes, my friend," said the financial brier bush. "You committed a misjudgment when you tried to lay hold of me. I lay hold of everyone myself."

It is a very good world to live in,
To lend, or to spend, or to give in,
But to beg or to borrow
Or to get a man's own,
It is the very worst world
That was ever known.

—John Wilmot, *Earl of Rochester*

MYOPIA

A middle management donkey and a top dog had attended a corporate meeting and were the last two animals to leave the conference room when they found a sealed document on the floor.

The donkey picked it up, broke the seal, unfolded the paper, and began to read it aloud. The document happened to point out business opportunities in different fodder markets: hay, barley, corn. Finding the advice not at all to his liking, the top dog said:

"Look a little further down, dear fellow. If you skip a bit, you may find something of value about the trade in meat and bones."

The donkey complied, and went through the whole report.

He did not find a single tip on the butcher business.

"Throw it away," barked the dog. "It is worthless nonsense."

While from the bounded level of our mind,
Short views we take, nor see the length Behind.

— Alexander Pope

I shoot the Hippopotamus
With bullets made of platinum
Because if I use leaden ones,
His hide is sure to flatten 'em.

— Hilaire Belloc

The vapor mild o'er each committee crept;
Unfinished business in each office slept.

— Alexander Pope

NEW AND UNIMPROVED PRODUCT PROLIFERATION

Abitch and a sow were both in charge of product development, the first for a company that developed sitcoms for TV networks, the second for a corporation that surprised consumers with ever newly packaged conditioners and shampoos.

One day these long acquainted professionals met at a convention that catered to creative brains across the board, from the whole spectrum of commerce and industry. Together, the pair listened to presentations about the failure of thousands of new products brought to market each year. Once the presentations were over, the two animals engaged in amiable shop talk.

The bitch claimed that she whelped new products more quickly than any other quadruped in the profession. "That's all very well," said the sow, "but allow me to point out that your puppies are blind when they are born."

What I like about this new stuff's nose dive,
Is that it's no longer alive.
There is a great deal to be said
For its being dead.

— *Edmund Clerihew Bentley*

Sir, there is no settling the precedence
Between a louse and a flea.

— *Samuel Johnson*

Oh, you sponges, brushes, combs,
Body lotions, shaving foams,
Grooming aids and eyebrow tweezers,
Eyelash teasers, pimple squeezers!

— *Wilhelm Busch, transl. Walter Arndt*

OFFICE POLITICS

Long ago, when Prometheus manufactured men, he decided to hang two bags from their necks, one in front filled with other people's defects, and a backpack behind them containing their own considerable shortcomings.

Almost at once, the new men invented office politics. No one waited for a fellow named Machiavelli, or for the author of Leadership Secrets of Attila the Hun and various similar tracts composed by the business fashion gurus of our own enlightened time. Oh no: the participants knew almost instantly how to play the game. They could see the faults of their rivals and co-workers from a mile away, but were unable to perceive their own. After all, their flaws were hidden behind their backs.

This splendid arrangement enables us mortals to this day to have great self-confidence. We certainly need it.

*I am thrifty. You're a bit of a tightwad. He's a real skinflint.
I'm cautious. You're timid. He's chicken-hearted.
I'm human. You're prone to err. He's a blundering idiot.
I have hepatitis. You drink too much. He's an alcoholic.
I'm human. You've got an eye for the girls, haven't you? He's lecherous.
I'm diplomatic. You take a pragmatic approach to the truth. He's a hypocrite.*

— David L. Silverman

*Psychologists of the utmost fame
Were called at once; but when they came,
They answered, as they took their fees,
There is no cure for this disease.*

— Hilaire Belloc

ON MANAGEMENT STYLES

The frogs were tired of dancing to the same old tune of a mildly autocratic boss and sent a deputation to Zeus to ask for a new leader. Zeus saw immediately how simple-minded these green little animals were.

But he decided to play along by dropping a block of wood in the company pond. At first, the frogs were frightened by the splash this made, and they fled out of sight into the darkest corners of their office cubicles at the bottom of the pond.

Yet gradually, because the block of wood stayed quite still, they came back to the water's surface. As the days and weeks went by, the frogs became so contemptuous of it, that they jumped up and squatted on the big piece of wood.

Thinking it undignified to be managed by such a touchy-feely wimp, a delegation of the frogs approached Zeus once more: this boss, they argued, was too easy-going and provided not the slightest challenge. Life at the office was simply boring. At that Zeus lost patience with the frogs. He told them they would get the management they deserved. So he presented them with a poisonous water snake.

*Look here, steward, if this is coffee,
I want tea; but if this is tea, then I wish for coffee.*

— Punch, 1902

*Oh, don't the days seem lank and long
When all goes right and nothing goes wrong,
And isn't your life extremely flat,
With nothing whatever to grumble at!*

— W. S. Gilbert

ON THE SHORTFALLS OF MANAGING BY OBJECTIVE

An ass, having the objective of crossing a river with a load of salt, lost his footing and slipped into the water so that the salt was dissolved. Having managed to reach his objective by finding himself expediently relieved of his burden, he was mightily pleased when he got upon his legs again.

So the next time an objective came along that needed to be managed, and as he reached the river with another load on his back, he remembered the first solution. Thinking that the same would happen if he went into the water to get his feet wet, the ass let himself go under on purpose. But this time he was loaded with sponges, which absorbed so much water that he could not keep his head up, grew confused, and drowned.

That so things are, and therefore so should be:
The proof inverted would be stronger far;
So they should be, and therefore so they are.
— *Alexander Pope*

The common cormorant or shag
Lay eggs inside a paper bag
The reason you will see no doubt
Is to keep the lightning out.

But what these unobservant birds
Have never noticed is that herds
Of wandering bears may come with buns
And steal the bags to hold the crumbs.
— *Anonymous*

The tools of working out salvation,
By mere mechanic operation.
—*Samuel Butler*

PAY FOR PERFORMANCE

At a gathering of corporate beasts a prominent monkey stood up and danced.

It was an outstanding, truly exceptional performance. Every dance step had been practiced and rehearsed until it seemed perfect and appeared to come easy. The audience applauded with such enthusiasm at this demonstration of elegance and competence, that a camel was jealous and desired to win similar recognition as an executive celebrity. So it got up and tried to dance like the monkey. But it made such a ridiculous spectacle of itself that the other conference animals cudgeled it out of their sight.

Darwinian Man, though well behaved,
At best is only a monkey shaved.

—W.S. Gilbert

Parody of a Roosevelt Speech:
At 3 o'clock on Saturday afternoon
Theodore Roosevelt will walk on the
Waters of Lake Michigan.
— Flyer distributed at
the Republican National Convention, 1912

The camel's hump is an ugly lump
Which well you may see at the Zoo;
But uglier yet is the hump we get
From having nothing to do.

— Rudyard Kipling

PERSONALITY CLASH

A tomcat wanted to find a plausible excuse to consume a fine cock who reported to him.

During the annual departmental performance review, the tomcat declared that the cock had made himself a nuisance to upper management by crowing at inopportune times, thereby preventing healthful executive sleep.

The cock defended himself by saying that he offered management a good service by waking it up to start a full day's work.

Then the cat charged him with being unduly friendly and indecent with his own mother and his sisters. The cock replied that this was strictly a case of love among the chickens, that it took place after business hours, and that it was a useful service to the company without costing it a penny simply because it increased the egg-laying productivity among the hens the employed by at this facility.

"You are full of vile and politically incorrect excuses," said the tomcat. "But that provides no reason why I should go hungry." So the cat made a meal out of the cock while serving his company loyally during a temporary period of consolidation.

*Cats come with mews,
All have sharp claws,
They air their views,
Stray soon from laws.*

— *J.A.Lindon*

*The rain it raineth on the just
And also on the unjust fella:
But chiefly on the just, because
The unjust steals the just's umbrella.*

— *Charles Bowen*

THE PRETENDER

A wolf thought that by disguising himself he could get a secure job and plenty to eat. Putting on a dress-for-success sheep skin to fool the animal-resources shepherd, he joined a flock at grass without being discovered.

Eventually the shepherd hired him; and after a time of probation, during which the wolf did all the right things, joined all the right organizations, and improved his savage table manners, he was shut in with the other sheep in the fold. Full of glee, the wolf anticipated feasts to come.

Then, feeling hungry for a good roast lamb dinner, the shepherd picked up a knife one day and selected one of his animals for supper.

It happened to be the wolf.

If all the good people were clever,
And all clever people were good,
The world would be nicer than ever,
We thought that it possibly could.

But somehow, 'tis seldom or never
The two hit it off as they should;
The good are so harsh to the clever,
The clever so rude to the good.

— Elizabeth Wordsworth

A sheep in sheep's clothing.

— Winston Churchill

THE PUBLIC'S IMAGE OF BUSINESS

Hermes, messenger of Zeus and god of trade and gain, was curious to find out how highly he was valued among the mortals. Taking the shape of a human being, he went to a sculptor's workshop and pretended to be an art lover.

On seeing a statue of Zeus, he inquired about its price. One hundred dollars, the sculptor said. Laughing, Hermes asked the same question about an image of Hera and was told that it was twice as expensive as the statue of Zeus. At length he noticed a sculpture of himself. Thinking that his importance in the scheme of things must cause him to be held in high esteem by the population, he asked: "And how much is the Hermes, god of trade and gain?" "Oh," replied the artist, if you buy the other two, I'll throw him in for nothing."

Who would be brave enough to dwell
On earth and walk this rut
If all of us resolved to tell
The truth and nothing but?

Then names would swarm on busy wings
Like scoundrel, hoodlum, skunk,
We'd tell each other awful things
Before we're even drunk.

I value graceful falsehood more,
The courtesy that eases,
I know the score, you know the score,
And every contact pleases.

— Wilhelm Busch, transl. Walter Arndt

RESTRUCTURING

An experienced old fox had for once been trapped in a deal and lost his fine, bushy tail as a result of it. Being a practical fellow who was determined to save face and much more, he saw no other choice but to persuade all the other foxes to maim themselves in the same way. Then, he reasoned, his own failure to hold on to his tail would be less conspicuous. Besides, he was accustomed to looking at the bright side and had already convinced himself that a case could be built for operating the business without tails.

So he called a meeting for all top executives and said: "As all of you who keep up with current trends know, divestures of marginal business units are the way to keep pace with volatile changes in the global economy. Our corporate mission needs re-thinking and updating. I propose that we divest ourselves of our tails. Tails are ugly, non-productive performers, they are detrimental to the bottom-line, and they are too heavy a burden to carry any longer. After these losers are gone, the company will be in a position to reinvest in core businesses that show excellent potential for sustainable future growth. To free assets, the tails must go. All department heads, and the entire corporation will gain by doing this. I expect total senior management involvement."

All the foxes agreed, except one. Said he "You only give us these marching orders because it suits your own book. Or could you tell me who is going to buy a bunch of tails? All this reshuffling and restructuring of businesses makes no sense, creates no value — not for companies, not for workers, and above all not for the economy as a whole. It only makes the lawyers and investment bankers rich. I propose we keep our tails and refrain from buying their dogs."

The Right Honorable Gentleman is indebted to his memory for his jests, and to his imagination for his facts.
— *R.B. Sheridan*

From oldest time he dealt in smoke;
Than smoke, no other thing he sold, or made;
Smoke all the substance of his stock in trade;
His capital all smoke, smoke all his store,
And many enter daily at his door!
— *Jacob Cats*

RÉSUMÉ EXPANSION

A lion's attention was attracted by a formidable résumé. By the sound and content of it, he thought it must come from some big, formidable and capable animal.

The lion followed a policy of hiring the best and the brightest for his company. After considering the résumé for a while, he decided to check the promising animal out by inviting it for lunch at his club.

Seeing and hearing that the applicant was a frog, the lion became unreasonably angry. He simply didn't believe the credentials and accomplishments listed in the résumé were real. He pretended to crush the frog with his paw and roared: "Imagine such a green, bloated little thing wasting my time and making such a noisy fuss!"

The frog by nature is both damp and cold,
His mouth is large, his belly much will hold;
He sits somewhat pretending, loves to be
Croaking in clubs and gardens, though unpleasantly.

— *John Bunyan*

We should console ourselves for the lack of great talents the same way as we do for the lack of high office: our good nature would unfit us for either of them.

— *Vauvenargues*

RETURN ON INVESTMENT

A tortoise, who was the president of a privately held company, and a hare, who was at the helm of a public company, started a dispute about which of them was more successful in generating earnings.

After arguing for hours without being able to reach an agreement, both executives decided that they would meet again in exactly ten years, compare performance, and settle the matter once and for all.

The hare had such confidence in his fleetness acquired by being under constant pressure to show excellent financial results in the short term, that he did not trouble himself about the long-term wager with the tortoise. We was certain that he would win the race simply by adding up all his outstanding short-term triumphs. After all, he had to win every quarterly and annual race against the bottom-line anyway, or else.

The tortoise, acutely aware that he was a much slower creature, and also aware that his company was closely held and that he could plan without the pressure of satisfying his shareholders (now called stakeholders) and Wall Street from quarter to quarter, padded along steadily without ever stopping.

Instead of outsourcing or producing abroad, he invested gradually and carefully in the best, most advanced equipment and technology money could buy, thereby increasing productivity in leaps and bounds. Instead of fattening many levels of a managerial hierarchy, the trained, treated, and compensated producers in manufacturing, quality control, sales, and customer service very well. In turn, his employees felt they worked for a good, democratic company and the customers responded by buying its well-made products: they even stopped to prefer imports. Before long, the tortoise developed a booming export business and was able to outperform foreign manufacturers and their cheaper labor. Shipping costs, and the energy usage associated with them, also declined considerably.

It had been a pain-staking process and did not happen overnight, But when the tortoise and the hare met again after ten years had gone by, it was simple to dissolve the dispute: the tortoise was clearly the winner.

"You had an unfair advantage," said the hare. "And you know what?

I am going to arrange a leveraged buy-out through our management. The first thing we will do after that will be to take the company private."

The tortoise had his doubts. He thought the whole thing was essentially a matter of attitude and mindset. But he said nothing.

Never do something you do not approve of in order more quickly to accomplish something you do approve of, for there are no safe short-cuts in piloting a business.
— J. Pierpont Morgan

*I know just how to cure the world
And make it safe and stable;
But I haven't time to do it,
And those that have, aren't able!*
— Leverett Lyon

*Time is the old justice that
Examines all offenders.*
— Shakespeare

RULES FOR DEALS

A lion, a donkey, and a fox formed a partnership and went out hunting for business success. When they had taken a good quantity of gamely profits, the lion told the donkey to share them out.

The donkey, who had a literal mind and was trained long before the Generally Accepted Accounting Principles became the subject of subtle interpretation, divided the profits into three equal parts and told the lion to choose one. On which the lion pounced on him in a fury, devouring him with zeal.

Next, the lion, most politely told the fox to divide the profits. The fox put nearly all of the earnings into one big pile and left only a small amount for himself. The then told the lion in his smoothest professional manner to kindly make his choice.

The lion congratulated the fox on his astute understanding of the unwritten business rules and inquired who had taught him to share game in the correct way. "The donkey," said the fox, "and what happened to him."

*A little stealing is a dangerous part,
But stealing largely is a noble art.
It's mean to rob a hen roost, or a hen,
But taking thousands makes us gentlemen."*
— Anonymous

*I am king of the Romans
And above Grammar.*
— Emperor Sigismund

SHARK REPELLENT

The management of a big corporation was fighting a hostile take-over attempt with no white knight in sight to come to the rescue.

Many of the stakeholders liked the inflated offer made by the raiders, and also the idea of showing professional management who was boss.

But one of the stakeholders objected. "Let me tell you a story," he said.

"A fox who was crossing a river was swept into a deep gully and all of his efforts to get out failed miserably. In addition to this dangerous predicament, he was also tormented by a swarm of ticks.

A hedgehog swimming that way on his travels was sorry for him and asked if he should pick off the ticks.

'No, please don't bother,' replied the fox.

'Why not?' inquired the hedgehog.

'Because these ticks have already satisfied their appetite on me, and don't suck much blood now.

But if you take them away, another lot will come, all hungry, and they will drain every drop of blood I have left.'"

"It's the same for us, my dear fellow stakeholders," said the speaker. "This crop of management will do no more harm, being already over-compensated as it is. But if you fall for the rhetoric of the raiders, other predatory animals will come who are still hungry; and they will begin anew to line their stomachs and their pockets out of the corporate coffers."

There are few ways in which a man can be more innocently employed than in getting money.
— *Samuel Johnson*

The race could save one-half its wasted labor Would each reform himself and spare his neighbor.
— *Putnam*

What is the opposite of doe? The answer's buck, as you should know. A buck _is_ doe, you say. Well, well, Clearly you don't know how to spell.

Moreover, get this through your head: The current slang for dough is bread.
— *Richard D. Wilbur*

SMALL CAN BE BEAUTIFUL

The small business mice, who were at war with the big business weasels, were always getting the worst of it.

One day they held the Small Business Conference of the Year and reached conclusions: they were always minding their own business, and consequently suffered from lack of leadership, lobbying power, and effective organization. Big business had all the clout, and unjustly so, since it was small business that created most of the new jobs.

So the mice elected a substantial number of generals with the mandate to work for improvement and returned well pleased to their little businesses.

Back home, they continued doing what they always did. They lived from minor crisis to minor crisis without the expert help of strategic planners, delegating whatever they could to ordinary employees with normal intelligence; they scrambled for business, managed scarce financial resources, and worked very long hours.

The new generals of the mice also returned home, but they recognized immediately that they needed to distinguish themselves from the rest of the small fry in order to accomplish something. Very quickly, they made horns and fixed them on their foreheads as symbols for the elevated rank and the fearsomeness they had acquired. The horns would certainly make them look more impressive, increase their stature, and project their determination in future dealings with the big business weasels.

Equipped with these large antlers, the generals of the mice started a whirlwind of activities. They harassed their local Chambers of Commerce to pay more than lip service to their community; they pestered politicians to represent them even without large campaign contributions; they organized meetings and seminars at the local level; they administered all these important events; and they talked, talked, talked — preparing for a showdown with the weasels. And all the while the generals were involved in a contradiction of survival terms for small business: they didn't have any time left to mind their own store.

When the mice finally joined battle with the weasels, their whole army was routed and took flight. All the lower ranks of the mice got safely into their little business holes except for the generals, who, unable to get in on account of their large horns, were caught and went bankrupt.

Hail, ye indominate heroes, hail!
Despite of all your generals ye prevail.

— *W.S. Landon*

The next time people ask you why you are tired, tell them. Your exhaustion is fully justified and you can prove it by a few simple statistics: The US has a population of over 200 million. Of these, 72 million are over 65, leaving 128 million to do the work. When you subtract that from the 75 million people under 21, you get 53 million. There are also 27.471,002 employed by the federal government in one capacity or another which leaves 25.528,998 to do the work. The 8 million in the armed forces leaves only 17.528,998 to do the work, and when you subtract from this the 15 million on state and city government payrolls, and the 1.520,00 in hospitals, mental institutions, and similar places, the work force is reduced to 1.008,998.

Fine, but there are an estimated 800,500 bums, vagrants, and others with a pathological fear of work. That leaves 208,498 people to carry the national workload, 208,496 of whom are presently behind bars. Which, brother, leaves you and me. And I don't know about you, but I am getting tired.

— Author unknown. His numbers are wildly wrong, but one can see his point.

STATE OF THE ECONOMY: THE PERENNIAL VIEW FROM MOUNT OLYMPUS

A busy elected representative decided that the time had come for him to pay respects to his constituents in the provinces. So he ventured down from the Hill and walked about to shake hands with voters. In due course, he also met with a group of local business people to discuss economic issues.

Said the first business creature:

"While I reject protectionism, unfair foreign dumping practices are quite another matter. Because of it, my industry suffers from unpleasantly heavy sweats."

"That's good" said the elected representative.

The second business creature, after listing a number of serious problems, stated: "All this has given my industry a shivering fit that has nearly shaken it to pieces."

"That's good too," said the elected representative.

The third business persona said: "Because of the merrily growing budget deficit, our industry has been diagnosed with a severe case of anemia."

"That's good once more," replied the politician, thanked the members of the business group for their time and informative contributions, and took himself off to settle down on Mount Olympus as before.

Returning from the meeting, the business creatures were asked about the outcome. "Well" one of them said, "if you ask me, there are a lot of clouds surrounding that Hill. Once you dwell there, these mists somehow produce an awesome 20/20 vision. As a result, the Hill-tenants see so many good symptoms among their constituents, that we might be just as well dead."

Men in high places, from having less personal interest in the characters of others — being safe from them — are commonly less acute observers, and with progressive elevation in life become, as more and more indifferent to what other men are, so more and more ignorant of them.
—Sir Henry Taylor

*Oh latest born and loveliest vision far —
Of all Olympus' faded hierarchy!*
— Keats

*Overwork: a dangerous disorder affecting
High public officials who want to go fishing.*
—Ambrose Bierce

STICK TO THE KNITTING

Lagging just a little behind the rest of the flock, a goat of a slightly different type found himself pursued by a wolf. Turning to him, the goat said: "I know very well that you are going to give me the ax. But I should like to perish with due ceremony. Please play the flute for me to dance. It is my last wish."

The wolf complied, and prudently called in the musicians from the humanoid services department for help and reinforcement. While the flute playing and dancing were going on, the merry music brought some law firm hounds and a few retrievers from the ACLU to the scene. Being chased by these hunting dogs, the wolf caught his breath and growled with indignation. "I got what I deserved," he said. "When I had messy work to do, I shouldn't have turned flute-player."

> But here the Turks were much mistaken
> Who, hating hogs, yet wished to save their bacon.
>
> — Byron

> Sometimes the monkey soul will sprawl
> Athwart the human eyes,
> And peering forth, will flesh its pads,
> And utter social lies.
>
> — Stevie Smith

STRATEGIC ALLIANCE

An ass and a fox read in the Wall Street Journal that strategic alliances can be a formula for success. So they held a meeting, decided to form a strategic alliance, discussed the possibility of a little harmless price-fixing, and went out to chase what was left of their competitors.

When a lion suddenly appeared in their path, the fox immediately realized the danger that threatened them. Approaching the lion with courage and decisiveness, he proposed a deal: he would hand over the ass for a guarantee of security. On receiving the lion's promise to honor this agreement, the fox lead the ass into a trap. But the lion, when he saw that the ass could not possible get out of the trap, seized the fox first and pursued the ass at his leisure.

*It is a double pleasure
To deceive the deceiver.*

— La Fontaine

*The statesman's art, that of fixn
Would have been more effective in Nixn
If he'd understood
That the bad and the good
Are for keeping apart, not for mixn.*

— Anonymous

TAX REFORM OR THE MOUNTAIN IN LABOR

The Hill above Washington was said to be in labor, and uttered the most dreadful cries.

The people, the lobbyists, and the representatives of interest groups gathered around the Hill to see what birth would be produced. While waiting, the people digested ten million words dealing with the matter, and the lobbyists, the media, and the interest group persons manufactured another ten million words, peddling their cases.

After everyone had waited a long time in great expectation for the labor to end, out crept a mouse.

Here comes Mr. Winter, Collector of Taxes
I advise you to give whatever he axes,
And that, too, without any nonsense and flummery
For, so his name's Winter, his actions are summary.

— Theodore Hook

He was in logic a great critic,
Profoundly skilled in analytic.
He could distinguish, and divide
A hair'twixt south and southwest side.
On either which he could dispute,
Confute, change hands, and still confute.

— Samuel Butler

POLITICAL OPPONENT'S MEASURE
2 nincompoops = 1 fathead
2 fatheads   = 1 incompetent
3 incompetents = 1 opportunist
2 opportunists =   1 Machiavelli

— Joe Ecclesine

One difference between a tax collector and
A taxidermist: the taxidermist leaves a hide.

— IRS Commissioner Mortimer Caplan

TRUTH IS TAKING A BATH

A salesman traveling through the desert had just passed the sleepy little town of Truth or Consequences in southern New Mexico, when he saw a lovely woman standing all alone in the middle of the sagebrush with her eyes bent to the ground. She was dressed in a white gown.

Astonished, he stopped his car and asked: "Who are you?"

"I used to be Truth" she answered. "But now, I don't know who I am any longer. So I am having an identity crisis and call myself Euphemism for the time being."

"And why have you left the world and the big cities to hide in this hot and remote place in the desert?"

"Because I do not feel so good. I need a rest, and I am taking the baths at the warm mineral springs in this town, trying to repair my health.

The name of this place attracted me. It's rather naïve, don't you think?"

The salesman didn't know how to answer this, so he said: "Does all this do you any good?"

"Some," she said, lifting her beautiful brown eyes. "Times have changed, as you know. In days gone by, lying was confined to a few. Now everybody does it but it is not called lying any longer. The age is far too sophisticated for that. There has been progress; I am one of the casualties. But because I have lived since the dawn of history, it would be ridiculous to assume that I could totally perish from future shock. That will not happen. I am a survivor and plan to outlive your era progress. Meanwhile, I will learn to adapt. I am trying to get used to my new name: Euphemism. It has a nice ring to it, don't you agree? Less despotic than truth."

"Well, I don't know" said the salesman, shifting his feet. He was getting sweltering in the heat, with the window of his car rolled down and the air-conditioning turned off.

"Goodness, perhaps the new name is rather bland," continued the woman. "I do miss the glorious days when men dared to say what they meant. If you had an enemy, you could insult him with gusto and grace. Grace was required: invective was an art. It was refreshing, I tell you! I felt alive, had some fun. But nowadays you have invented such a miserable diet of strategic misrepresentations that I don't know the truth anymore."

The traveler needed to get away. He murmured a good luck towards the phantom in the desert, pushed a button to roll up his window, and drove off as fast as he could.

*It cannot in the opinion of His Majesty's
Government be classified as slavery in the
extreme acceptance of the word without some
risk of terminological inexactitude.*
— Winston Churchill

*The man who could call a spade a spade should
be compelled to use one. It is the only thing he is fit for.*
— Oscar Wilde

*Truth is such a precious article, let us all
economize in its use.*
— Mark Twain

WASTE OF TALENT

An enterprising man well suited to the martial art of doing business had a horse which, as long as he was at war building his company, shared all his dangers and adventures and was well fed on the fine barley of appreciation.

But when the wars were over, the horse was appointed Vice President of Humanoid Resources, carried token loads, and was being fed on nothing but chaff.

War was declared again, and when the trumpets sounded the soldier-founder of the company bridled his horse, armed himself, and mounted. But the horse had lost its spunk and said to him: "You had better go and join an infantry regiment, for I am not worth to be called a war horse now. You have turned me into a donkey. How can you expect to change me back again?"

My salad days,
When I was green in judgment.

— *Shakespeare*

Absence of proper occupation is no rest.
A mind quite vacant is a mind distress'd.

— *Cowpter*

Horse sense is what keeps horses from
betting what people will do.

— *Anonymous*

If you enjoyed your reading, please take a few moments and leave a a review via the link at the bottom of the book's Amazon page. It helps the algorithm! Thank you.

Acknowledgements

Every effort has been made to locate parties who hold rights to excerpts reprinted here. I thankfully acknowledge the following permissions:

Kenneth Burke, "In a world full of problems, he sat doing puzzles" from Collected Poems 19161967. Copyright © 1968 by the Regents of the University of California. Reprinted by permission of the University of California Press.

Wilhelm Busch, excerpts translated by Walter Arndt, from The Genius of Wilhelm Busch: Comedy of Frustration: An English Anthology, edited and translated by Walter Arndt (Berkeley: University of California Press, 1982). Reprinted with the permission of the translator.

Willard R. Espy, excerpt from "School=s Out" Another Almanac of Words at Play (New York: Clarkson Potter, 1980). Copyright © 1980 by Willard R. Espy. Reprinted with the permission of Harold Ober Associates, Incorporated.

Richard Wilbur, "What is the opposite of doe?" from Opposites: Poems and Drawings. Copyright © 1973 by Richard Wilbur. Reprinted by permission of Houghton Mifflin Harcourt Publishing Company.

About The Author

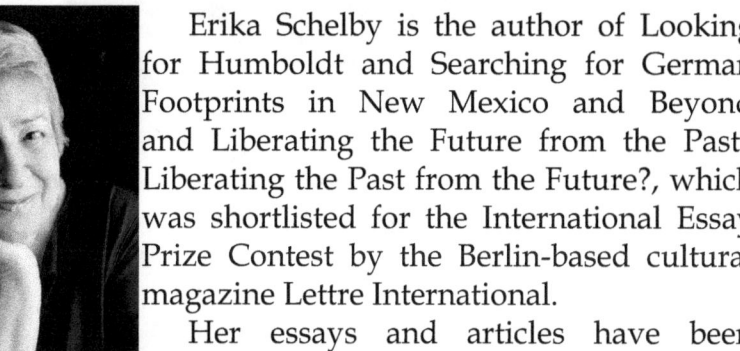

Erika Schelby is the author of Looking for Humboldt and Searching for German Footprints in New Mexico and Beyond and Liberating the Future from the Past? Liberating the Past from the Future?, which was shortlisted for the International Essay Prize Contest by the Berlin-based cultural magazine Lettre International.

Her essays and articles have been published by the International Media Institute NYC, and in Salon; AlterNet; Pressenza International Press Agency; Asia Times; Counter Punch; History News Network; L.A.Progressive; Nation Of Change; Citizen Truth; News Click; and more.

Erika Schelby is a writer with much experience in business. She co-owned and team-built a small design-focussed company, worked in management positions in Europe and the United States, traveled widely, and holds a B.A. (Phi Beta Kappa) and a M.S. degree from American Universities. She lives in New Mexico and likes the state's environment and culture..

Website: https://lookingforhumboldt.com

www.ingramcontent.com/pod-product-compliance
Lightning Source LLC
Chambersburg PA
CBHW060517030426
42337CB00015B/1917